Cosmic Evanescence

Colin Martin

BookLeaf Publishing

Presentation by *BookLeaf Publishing*

Web: www.bookleafpub.com

E-mail: info@bookleafpub.com

ISBN: 9789357441216

First edition 2023

DEDICATION

To all my dear friends and family, who give me life and constantly inspire me

ACKNOWLEDGEMENT

A special thank you to Dave Barney for his guidance, mentorship, and friendship

Genesis

Creativity is an impulse
As natural as breathing
Ideas as plentiful as air

Melodies, letters, sonic colors
Cascade in my brain like raindrops
In a magical monsoon

Dances of joy
Songs of sorrow
Words of wonder

Playground

As the children ran screaming we sat on the jungle gym, alone
Imagining ourselves as wizards
Monsters
Heroes

We cared not for the
Strictness of the steel slide,
The severity of the sand.

Youth was a gift.
If only we knew to savor it.

Shatter

Memories often vanish,
Victim to the years.
We always remember our first heartbreak,
though:

That moment when ethereal ecstasy
Twists to tortured turmoil
Melts to maddening misery
Rips to ravaged ruin
Leaves us lying
Breathless, bleak, bitter
Under the weeping willow

Reverie

They say that the grass is always greener on the other side
and they're right.

In youth we yearn to ripen
and now as we decay
we covet the days
where we ignored the teacher's monotone
and dreamt of Spanish gardens
Guitars
Sweetness of feminine nectar

Krom

In a bygone age
Now a rose-colored haze
We were teenagers
Drunk on hormones
Eating bread and drinking soda
Sitting on gypsum rocks watching the crimson summer sunset's
Ephemeral brilliance mirror our own.

The days were all too brief when
The past was nothing but an afterthought
The future was intangible mystery of perfection
And we honestly believed we were more than
Dust
In the infinity of time

The Swim Meet

Immaculate stillness of anticipation
Leading to explosive power
Fury of motion
Water roaring into a white thunder

How rare it is
How precious
To be able to unleash one's heart
In the name of victory
Eternal glory
Love
Family

The Concert

Silence
Erupting into chaos
Timbres
Colors
Oceans of sound
Coalescing into
Sublime apotheosis

Nocturne I

Crisp urgency of dry air
Ripe with the life of summer
The pulse of a thousand crickets

I trod with deliberate footsteps
My thoughts consumed with wonder
Under a million impossible stars.

My mind murmurs melodies of Mendelssohn.

What of tomorrow?
Is there a golden girl of the future?
Have I already met her?

Thoughts of past, present, beautiful future
All perfectly unifying
Into a divine
White-hot
Now

Haiku I

It's not as they say:
Rainy days do not always
Yield to sunny skies

Vermont

As the flakes flurry
And the earth hardens into bitter ice
I lie on my cruel mattress
Listening to the raucous rat-a-tat of my heart
As I grieve my failures
Burdens
Soul-swallowing seclusion

Then I remind myself:
There is beauty in uncertainty
Solitude
Silence of snowfall

Perchance to Dream

A pandemonium of pinball thoughts
Cascading in effervescent entropy
Breaking, smashing, uniting in piecemeal
Into steady singularity

Swarms of melting green
Descend to red
Dissolve to black
And into
Blissful oblivion

Divinity

I always wanted to be a God
Flawless
Superior
Dominant

But all along all I really wanted
Was to be loved

Haiku II

Come and dance with me
In the spring rain. Like the Earth,
We can be reborn.

The Cellist

Golden glimmer of sun-splashed syllables
Dancing in dulcet tones
Of lilting laughter
Flowering friendship
Jingling joy

The bliss of black coffee
Black hair
Bay skies of baby blue

Urban Isolation

Grey dawn
Damp with dreary drops
Blurs in a bleary blue.
San Francisco stirs.

I have risen before the city,
Muffled footsteps the soundtrack
To my savored solitude.

My joy, my lovely loneliness
Is as the fragility of fog
Floating, fading to
Fiery daylight.

Tinder Haikus

Staring into screens
Swiping left, right, endlessly
Yearning dopamine.

A world of lost souls
Raised upon lies of romance
Craving connection.

Here they will find none.
All they'll find is emptiness,
Digital despair.

Rue

How it still lingers
In the corners of my brain
The stench of sweat
Intimacy
Regret

If I saw you again
After all these years
Would you even remember my name

Nocturne II

Every night I set out traps for the ghosts of my past.

Sometimes they visit me in dreams.
Long lost lovers
Former friends
Visions of who I was supposed to be.

They beckon to me to follow them. I cannot.
I can only wake to the starkness of sweat
Thirst
Cold dawn

Eternity

Nobody is immune to tragedy.

We're always blindsided at the moment of
reckoning
An accident
Disease
Violence
An overdose

We all think ourselves immortal on warm spring
afternoons
Drinking juice
Under impossibly blue skies

Panacea

You considered your emotions as merely
chemicals
Numbers, reactions, data
A flaw to be easily rectified
With the simple swallow of a pill.

But for all your brilliance
You could never learn
That no pill can ever cure
Loneliness.

Coda

I will mourn the art I cannot create.

Alas, there are only so many melodies
So many words
So many hours
In our cosmic evanescence

www.ingramcontent.com/pod-product-compliance
Lightning Source LLC
Chambersburg PA
CBHW051719130826
49812CB00034B/1260
9789357441216